FANTASTIC SPORT FACTS

FOOTBALL

Michael Hurley

Raintree

H00
Sch
D0320276

Raintree is an imprint of Capstone Global Library Limited, a company incorporated in England and Wales having its registered office at 7 Pilgrim Street, London, EC4V 6LB – Registered company number: 6695582

www.raintreepublishers.co.uk
myorders@raintreepublishers.co.uk

Text © Capstone Global Library Limited 2013
First published in hardback in 2013
First published in paperback in 2014
The moral rights of the proprietor have been asserted.

All rights reserved. No part of this publication may be reproduced in any form or by any means (including photocopying or storing it in any medium by electronic means and whether or not transiently or incidentally to some other use of this publication) without the written permission of the copyright owner, except in accordance with the provisions of the Copyright, Designs, and Patents Act 1988 or under the terms of a licence issued by the Copyright Licensing Agency, Saffron House, 6–10 Kirby Street, London EC1N 8TS (www.cla.co.uk). Applications for the copyright owner's written permission should be addressed to the publisher.

Edited by Catherine Veitch, Sian Smith, and John-Paul Wilkins
Designed by Richard Parker
Picture research by Ruth Blair
Originated by Capstone Global Library Ltd
Printed and bound in China

ISBN 978 1 406 25346 7 (hardback)
16 15 14 13 12
10 9 8 7 6 5 4 3 2 1

ISBN 978 1 406 25352 8 (paperback)
17 16 15 14 13
10 9 8 7 6 5 4 3 2 1

British Library Cataloguing in Publication Data
Hurley, Michael.
Football. -- (Fantastic sport facts)
796.3'34-dc23
A full catalogue record for this book is available from the British Library.

Acknowledgements
We would like to thank the following for permission to reproduce photographs: Corbis p. 16 (© Don Mason); Getty Images pp. 5 (Michael Steele), 6 (Darren England), 7 (Hamish Blair), 8 (Bob Thomas), 9, 19 (Stephen Dunn), 10 (MAURICIO LIMA/AFP), 11 (DANIEL ROLAND/ AFP), 12 (Ben Radford/ALLSPORT), 13 (Phil Cole), 14, 22 (Popperfoto), 17 (Alex Livesey), 20 (GIANLUIGI GUERCIA/ AFP); Photoshot pp. 15, 24 (© Imago), 18 (© Picture Alliance); Shutterstock pp. 4 (© Vladimir Melnik), 14 (© Booka), 17 (© Tatiana Popova), 21 (© Aptyp_koK), 21 (© Cory Thoman), 23 (© sportgraphic), 25 (© Natursports), 26 (© Photo Works); Superstock p. 27 (© Jonathan Larsen / age footstock).

Cover photograph of Marta of Brazil reproduced with permission of Getty Images (Scott Heavey), and a football reproduced with permission of Shutterstock (© Aptyp_koK).

Every effort has been made to contact copyright holders of any material reproduced in this book. Any omissions will be rectified in subsequent printings if notice is given to the publisher.

Disclaimer
All the internet addresses (URLs) given in this book were valid at the time of going to press. However, due to the dynamic nature of the internet, some addresses may have changed, or sites may have changed or ceased to exist since publication. While the author and publisher regret any inconvenience this may cause readers, no responsibility for any such changes can be accepted by either the author or the publisher.

HAMPSHIRE SCHOOLS LIBRARY SERVICE
WITHDRAWN

H005109099	
Askews & Holts	18-Mar-2014
796.33	£7.99

Contents

Some words are printed in bold, **like this**. You can find out what they mean by looking in the glossary.

Football around the world

Football is the world's most popular sport. The best footballers play in the top football leagues around the world.

The World Cup takes place every four years. It attracts fans from all over the world.

DID YOU KNOW?

Brazil has won the World Cup five times. That is more than any other country.

Goal rush

The record for the highest score ever in a football match was set in 2001. In a World Cup qualifying match, Australia beat American Samoa 31 – 0.

American Samoa didn't win a match until 2011 – 10 years later!

RECORD BREAKERS

Archie Thompson set the record for most goals scored by a single player in the same game. He scored an incredible 13 goals!

Young and old

The youngest footballer to ever play at the World Cup is Norman Whiteside. He was only 17 years and 41 days old when he played for Northern Ireland in 1982.

Roger Milla is the oldest World Cup player, at 42 years and 39 days. He played for Cameroon at the 1994 World Cup.

Roger Milla is joined by a teammate as he celebrates after scoring against Russia.

Goal-scoring goalkeeper!

Brazilian goalkeeper Rogerio Ceni does more than just stop the **opposition** from scoring. He holds the record for the most goals scored by a goalkeeper. He's scored over 100 goals!

DID YOU KNOW?

Hope Solo is the goalkeeper for the United States women's team. She was not always a goalkeeper. In high school, she played as a **striker** and scored over 100 goals!

Penalty nightmares

Penalties look easy, but there is a lot of pressure on penalty takers. In the 1994 World Cup final, Italian superstar Roberto Baggio missed the final penalty in the shootout to hand the win to Brazil.

Baggio was devastated after missing his penalty.

At the **Copa America** in 1999, Argentina **striker** Martin Palermo missed three penalties in the same match.

DID YOU KNOW?

After the **tournament** ended, Palermo did not play for his country again for 10 years!

Fastest goals ever

Turkey's Hakan Sukur holds the record for the fastest goal scored at the World Cup. He took just 11 seconds to score!

RECORD BREAKERS

The fastest goal scored in a World Cup final was scored by Johan Neeskens for the Netherlands. He took 90 seconds to score against West Germany in 1974.

Bees stop play!

During a match between Vista Hermosa and Alianza FC in El Salvador in 2011, a swarm of bees stopped play. The players had to run for shelter or lie down on the pitch!

DID YOU KNOW?

In 2012, during a Premier League match between Everton and Manchester City, a fan handcuffed himself to the goalpost! The match had to be stopped while he was removed from the pitch.

The top goal scorer at each World Cup wins the **Golden Boot** award.

Just Fontaine, of France, holds the record for the most goals scored at one World Cup. He scored an incredible 13 goals in 1958.

The record for the most goals scored in one match at the World Cup is held by Russia's Oleg Salenko. He scored five against Cameroon in 1994.

Golden Boot winners at the last three World Cups:

Year	Player	Country	Goals
2010	Mueller	Germany	5
2006	Klose	Germany	5
2002	Ronaldo	Brazil	8

Giant ball

The largest ever football was made for the 2010 World Cup in South Africa. The ball takes three hours to **inflate**! It is over 70 times the size of a normal football and weighs 1,500 times more!

DID YOU KNOW?

Pigs' bladders were used as balls until the first football was made by Charles Goodyear in 1855.

Oldest professional team

Notts County is the oldest **professional** football club in the world. The club was started in 1862. In 1888, it was one of the 12 professional clubs that set up the Football League in England.

DID YOU KNOW?

Italian giants Juventus modelled their kit on Notts County's kit. They have won the Italian league 28 times!

Great players

Pele scored over 1,000 goals during his career!

Pele is one of the greatest footballers of all time. He helped Brazil to win an amazing three World Cups (in 1958, 1962, and 1970).

DID YOU KNOW?

Lionel Messi plays for Barcelona and Argentina. He scored a record 82 goals for his club and country during the 2011-2012 season.

David Beckham is one of the most famous footballers in the world. He is known for his skill at taking **free kicks**.

David Beckham uses a special **technique** to strike the ball.

DID YOU KNOW?

Marta Viera da Silva, known as Marta, plays for Brazil. She won the **FIFA World Player of the Year** award five times in a row between 2006 and 2010.

Quiz

Are you a superfan or a couch potato? Decide whether the statements below are true or false. Then look at the answers on page 31 and check your score on the fanometer.

1 Brazil has won the World Cup the most times.

2 Australia's national football team is known as the Socceroos.

3 During a match a player can run over 11.2 kilometres (7 miles).

TOP TIP
Some of the answers can be found in this book, but you may have to find some yourself.

4 In 1999, Martin Palermo missed two **penalties** in the same match for Argentina.

5 Lionel Messi scored 62 goals for Barcelona and Argentina during the 2011-2012 season.

6 The first football was created in 1955.

FANOMETER

all-rounder

couch potato

superfan

1 2 3 4 5 6

Glossary

Copa America tournament for South American national teams that takes place every four years

FIFA World Player of the Year annual award given to the football player judged to have played the best

free kick free kick of the ball, awarded when the opposition breaks the rules

Golden Boot award given to the top scorer in each World Cup

inflate fill something with air, or gas, so that it swells up

opposition team that you are playing against

penalty free shot at goal from 12 yards. Only the goalkeeper can defend a penalty.

professional doing a job as a way of earning money

striker attacking player who tries to score goals

technique special way of doing something

tournament competition where there is a series of games or contests

Find out more

Books

The Kingfisher Football Encyclopedia,
Clive Gifford (Kingfisher, 2010)

FIFA World Football Records 2012,
Keir Radnedge (Carlton Books Ltd, 2011)

Websites

pbskids.org/kws/sports
Find out more about your favourite
sports, including tips on how to play.

**www.premierleague.com/en-gb/
kids.html**
Watch videos, find out the latest news,
and play online soccer games here.

Quiz answers

1) True. Brazil has won the World Cup five times (see page 5).
2) True.
3) True.
4) False. Palermo missed three penalties in the match (see page 13).
5) False. Messi scored 82 goals for Barcelona and Argentina during the 2011–2012 season (see page 25).
6) False. The first football was created in 1855 (see page 21).

Index